W9-BJN-767

Fossils

ANN O. SQUIRE

Children's Press®
An Imprint of Scholastic Inc.
New York Toronto London Auckland Sydney
Mexico City New Delhi Hong Kong
Danbury, Connecticut

Content Consultant
Elizabeth A. Nesbitt, PhD
Curator of Paleontology, Burke Museum
Associate Professor, Earth & Space Sciences Department
University of Washington
Seattle, Washington

Library of Congress Cataloging-in-Publication Data

Squire, Ann.
  Fossils/by Ann O. Squire.
    p. cm.—(True book)
  Includes bibliographical references and index.
  Audience: Grades 4–6.
  ISBN-13: 978-0-531-26142-2 (lib. bdg.) — ISBN-13: 978-0-531-26250-4 (pbk.)
1. Fossils—Juvenile literature. I. Title.
  QE714.5.S65 2012
  560—dc23   2012000649

© 2013 Scholastic Inc.

All rights reserved. Published in 2013 by Children's Press, an imprint of Scholastic Inc.
Printed in the United States of America. 113
SCHOLASTIC, CHILDREN'S PRESS, A TRUE BOOK™, and associated logos are trademarks and/or registered trademarks of Scholastic Inc.
8 9 10 R 22 21 20 19 18 17

Front cover:
Tyrannosaurus rex **skeleton**
Back cover: Trilobite fossil

Find the Truth!

Everything you are about to read is true *except* for one of the sentences on this page.

Which one is **TRUE**?

T or F Scientists can learn about all the world's extinct animals by studying fossils.

T or F Dinosaurs had been extinct for more than 60 million years before humans first developed.

Find the answers in this book.

Contents

THE **BIG** TRUTH!

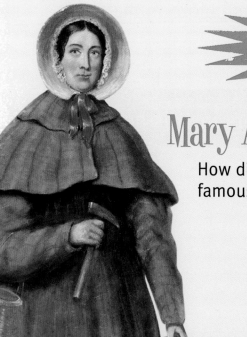

Mary Anning, Fossil Hunter

Paleontologists dig up an ancient rhinocerous skeleton.

Fuels from ancient fossils supply many of our energy needs today.

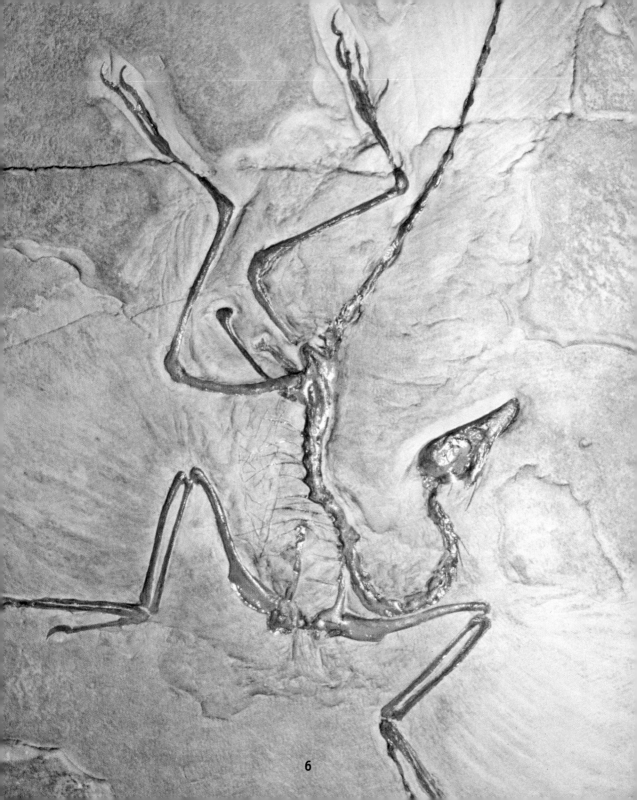

CHAPTER 1

Clues From the Past

Did you ever wonder how scientists have learned so much about Earth's history? How do we know what the dinosaurs looked like, what they ate, or where they lived? How do we know that fish existed before mammals? How have we learned about our human ancestors? The answer to these questions is through the study of **fossils**. Fossils are the remains, or traces, of animals and plants that have been preserved in the earth's rocky crust.

 *Archaeopteryx is considered the earliest bird.*

Digging Up Fossils

Most fossils are buried beneath the earth. **Paleontologists** excavate, or dig and remove, them from the surrounding rock. Fossils are delicate, so scientists must work carefully. Excavators may mist water on the rock to soften it. Then they use tools such as dental picks to chip the rock away. Large bones are usually encased in plaster of Paris to protect them for transport. They are shipped to laboratories for further study.

Paleontologists carefully excavate a 10-million-year-old rhinoceros skeleton in Nebraska.

The Hadrosaurus lived in what is now New Jersey.

This fossil shows the scaly skin of a *Hadrosaurus*.

Bones and More

When you think of a fossil, you probably picture a dinosaur bone or even a complete skeleton. But fossils can be more than just bones. Teeth, shells, and other hard parts of plants and animals can also become fossils. Sometimes, an animal leaves behind traces such as footprints, tooth marks, or even impressions of its skin. Clear fossil impressions of dinosaur skin give us a good idea of what these ancient animals looked like.

Ancient worms created these tracks in the earth, which later fossilized.

Another thing that animals leave behind is their droppings. Fossilized droppings are called coprolites. They can tell us a lot about an animal's size and what the animal ate. Worms and other soft animals cannot become fossils, but the burrows they dig can become fossilized. By looking at the space in which an animal lived, we can learn a lot about its size and shape.

Fossils Young and Old

Life has existed on Earth for billions of years. So a 10,000-year-old fossil is actually very young. Animals preserved during Earth's last ice age are among the youngest fossils ever found. Scientists in Australia recently discovered fossils that may be the world's oldest. These fossilized single-celled organisms are 3.4 billion years old!

Special lighting and powerful microscopes help paleontologists look at fossilized single-celled organisms, such as algae, shown here.

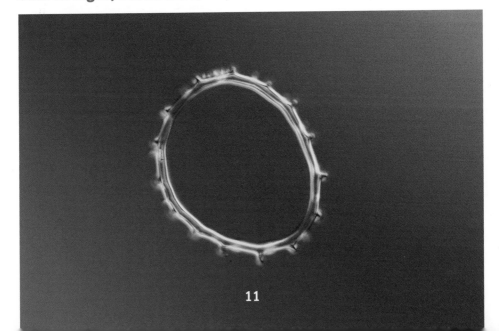

Earth was formed 4.6 billion years ago. At first, conditions were harsh and very hot. The air had no oxygen. Around 540 million years ago, animals that we might recognize began to develop. This was the beginning of the Paleozoic era. Sponges, worms, and snails were among the first animals. Fish developed around 400 million years ago, followed by insects and amphibians. In the middle of the Paleozoic era, 310 million years ago, reptiles developed.

The first trilobites lived on Earth about 542 million years ago.

Scientists argue that brachiosaurs lived in groups.

Ruling Reptiles

The Mesozoic era came next, lasting from 250 million to 65 million years ago. Reptiles dominated the land, overshadowing all other animals. In fact, this era is often called the age of reptiles. Dinosaurs such as *Tyrannosaurus rex*, *Stegosaurus*, and *Triceratops* roamed the earth at various times during this period. Yet the age of reptiles did not last forever. By the end of the Mesozoic era, all the dinosaurs had become **extinct**.

Giant mammoths and dire wolves lived about 150 thousand years ago.

The Age of Mammals

After the dinosaurs became extinct, mammals developed rapidly, replacing the ruling reptiles on land. This age of mammals, from 65 million years ago until the present, is known as the Cenozoic era. Giant mastodons and saber-toothed cats were some of the animals that lived during this time. The first modern humans developed very recently—only about 200,000 years ago!

What Are Fossil Fuels?

Fossils provide much of the energy we use today. Coal, oil, and natural gas are called **fossil fuels**. Hundreds of millions of years ago, wet tropical areas filled with plants and animals covered much of the earth. When organisms died, they sank to the bottom of the swamps, oceans, and bogs. They were buried under layers of sand and clay. Over millions of years, heat and pressure in the earth's crust transformed the matter into coal, oil, and natural gas.

Huge drilling rigs pump oil from deep within the Earth.

CHAPTER 2

Preserved in Stone

We know that fossils are usually excavated from layers of rock. But how did they get there? The material surrounding the fossil didn't start out as rock. In fact, most fossils were formed underwater or in places where the ground was wet and soft. The process of **fossilization** begins when a plant or animal dies and is quickly covered up by layers of mud or sand. Let's take a look at an example of how this happens.

Fossilized footprints tell us that this desert was once a soft, wet swamp.

Becoming a Fossil

Some 200 million years ago, a shallow ocean covered what is now California. A fish living in the ocean died and sank to the bottom. Before another animal had a chance to eat it, the fish was covered by a thin layer of sand. Over time, layers of sand and mud piled on top of the fish's body, burying it deep under the ocean floor. The skin and soft parts of the fish decayed, leaving only the skeleton behind.

To become a fossil, a fish would have to be quickly buried before any other marine animals tried to eat it.

Some of today's deserts were once covered by oceans and lakes.

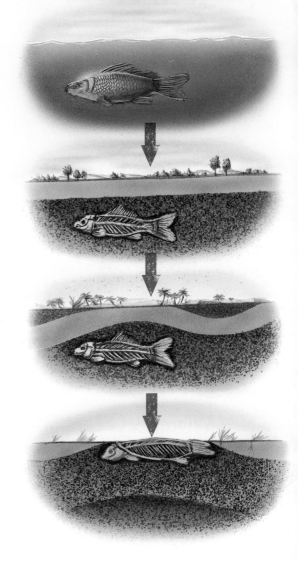

A skeleton is fossilized after spending millions of years under the earth.

After millions of years, there were many, many layers of sand covering the fish. The pressure from the upper layers was so great that the lower layers hardened into rock. The bones of the fish were trapped inside the rock. As water seeped through tiny cracks and spaces in the rock, it dissolved minerals in the fish's bones. Other, harder minerals replaced them. The result was a **petrified** fossil of the fish's skeleton.

Sometimes several fossilized fish or other animals are found together.

Finding Fossils

Millions of years later, Earth's climate has changed and portions of the ocean have dried up. Earthquakes altered the landscape, bringing deep layers of rock to the surface. Rocks that were once at the bottom of an ocean are now pushed up to form a mountain range. Present-day paleontologists excavating a California hillside are thrilled. They find the perfectly preserved skeleton of the fish that sank to the bottom of the sea all those years ago.

Lost in Time

We learn a lot about extinct animals and plants by studying their fossils. By examining dinosaur fossils, scientists have learned how large these reptiles were and how they walked. They also discovered what dinosaurs ate and what their skin texture was like. Is it possible to find out this much about every animal that lived during prehistoric times? Unfortunately, the answer is no.

Tracks can tell us how an animal walked and how fast it moved.

Without a Trace

It is not easy to become a fossil, and many animals never get the chance. Fossils are usually, though not always, the preserved hard parts of an animal—its bones, teeth, or shell. Soft-bodied animals such as slugs, worms, jellyfish, and octopuses have no hard parts to leave behind. Most of these animals have vanished from Earth's history without a trace.

There are more than 1,500 species of jellyfish.

Animals such as jellyfish have no hard parts that can fossilize.

Even well-preserved skeletons are rarely complete. Scientists use clues from similar fossils to learn about missing pieces.

Even animals with bones do not always become fossils. To become a fossil, the body must be covered up very quickly after death. In most cases, that doesn't happen. After an animal dies, another animal may eat its body. Its bones may be chewed up or scattered. The animal's body may also decompose, or rot. There are many extinct animals and plants we will never know about because they didn't leave fossils behind.

This prehistoric fly was found trapped in amber excavated in Lithuania.

CHAPTER 3

A Sticky Situation

There are other ways in which fossils can form. In some cases, animals became trapped in tar, ice, or sticky tree sap. These materials can create an even more interesting fossil than one excavated from layers of rock. Skin, hair, and other soft parts that would normally decay are often preserved. As a result, scientists can see exactly what these animals looked like.

Hardened tree sap is sometimes used to make jewelry.

Deep Freeze

If you've ever heated up a frozen pizza, you know that cold is a good way to preserve food. Intense cold can also preserve animals. Mammoths dating back 10,000 to 30,000 years have been found buried in ice in Alaska and Siberia. Despite their age, these animals were found in good condition. Their hair, skin, bones, muscles, and internal organs were intact. In some cases, the remains of their last meal were still in the stomach!

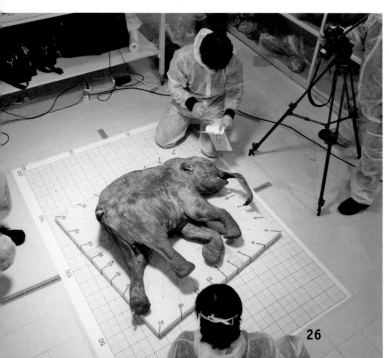

Scientists found traces of its mother's milk in this baby mammoth's stomach.

A whole insect preserved in amber is a rare and valuable find.

Stuck in Sap

Ancient pine trees, just like those of today, gave off a sticky sap. Sometimes small animals—such as insects, spiders, or lizards—stepped in the oozing sap and got stuck. More layers of sap eventually covered them completely. When the sap hardened over time, the bodies of these unlucky animals were perfectly preserved. The brownish-yellow fossilized sap is called amber. Scientists have found amber that contains insects and lizards that lived 40 million years ago.

More than three million fossils have been excavated from the La Brea Tar Pits.

The La Brea Tar Pits

Near the skyscrapers of downtown Los Angeles, California, are several small lakes. These are no ordinary lakes. They are filled with tar, which has been oozing out of the ground for thousands of years. Much of the tar has hardened. In the late 1800s, people noticed that the hardened tar contained bones. Scientists looked at the bones and found that they belonged to an extinct sloth that lived thousands of years earlier.

The La Brea Tar Pits contain the preserved bones of many different animals. The bones give scientists a good picture of life in the region tens of thousands of years ago. Scientists argue that thirsty animals were attracted to rainwater that collected on the tar's surface. Many animals became trapped in the tar as they drank. Struggling to free themselves, they attracted wolves, saber-toothed cats, and other **predators**, who often became trapped as well.

Many animals were caught and preserved in the La Brea Tar Pits.

Mary Anning, Fossil Hunter

Mary Anning was born in 1799 in Lyme Regis on the southern coast of England. To make extra money, her father searched the seaside cliffs for fossils to sell. Each winter, fierce storms battered the cliffs, wearing away layers of rock and exposed fossils buried within. He often took Mary and her brother, Joseph, on his trips. After her father died, 11-year-old Mary continued fossil hunting on her own.

In 1810, Mary surprised everyone by unearthing the skeleton of an *Ichthyosaurus*, a large marine reptile from the Jurassic period. She later discovered skeletons of *Plesiosaurus*, another marine reptile, and *Pterosaurus*, a flying reptile.

Fossil hunting was a dangerous job. In 1833, a landslide killed Mary's dog, Tray. Mary barely escaped. She continued to excavate fossils throughout her life and became one of the best-known fossil hunters of her time.

Paleontologists take a break during an excavation near the South Pole.

CHAPTER 4

Here, There, and Everywhere

When you think of a team of paleontologists digging for fossils, you might picture a remote mountain range or a windswept desert. But fossils have been found almost everywhere on Earth, even north of the Arctic Circle and near the South Pole. Wherever you live, there is a good chance that scientists have found fossils nearby.

Antarctica was not covered with snow and ice during the Mesozoic era.

Paleontologists working in the western and central parts of the United States and Canada have found lots of dinosaur bones. One of the best sites is in Utah at Dinosaur National Monument, where dinosaur fossils have been found in rock layers dating back 150 million years. *Tyrannosaurus rex*, *Triceratops*, and *Stegosaurus* bones have been found in Colorado and other western states. Dinosaur tracks have been found in many places, including Massachusetts and New York.

Timeline of Life on Earth

4.6 billion years ago
Earth forms as a solid planet.

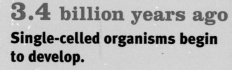

3.4 billion years ago
Single-celled organisms begin to develop.

400 million years ago
The first sharks develop in the oceans.

Layers of Rock

Most fossils are formed when layers of sediment build up. The rock that is created by these layers is called **sedimentary rock**. Sedimentary rock is recognizable by its crosswise layers. Each layer comes from sediment that built up and turned to stone millions of years ago. One place to see sedimentary rock layers is the Grand Canyon in Arizona. Paleontologists have unearthed algae, coral, and other early marine fossils there.

230 million years ago
The first dinosaurs develop.

65 million years ago
Dinosaurs go extinct; mammals become more dominant on land.

Scientists originally thought the *Basilosaurus* was a reptile. Even though it is a mammal, its name means "king lizard!"

Know Your State Fossil!

Did you know that many U.S. states have a state fossil? Utah's is the *Allosaurus*, a fierce, 3-ton dinosaur from the Jurassic period. Some 8,000 *Allosaurus* fossils have been excavated from a single site in Utah. Alabama's state fossil is the *Basilosaurus*, a fish-eating whale that lived more than 45 million years ago. New York's state fossil is a sea scorpion that is more than 400 million years old. What's your state fossil?

Return of the Woolly Mammoth

Can an extinct species be brought back to life? Some scientists believe so. Paleontologists recently uncovered a woolly mammoth preserved perfectly in the frozen soil of Siberia. Using **DNA** from the mammoth's thighbone, researchers hope to **clone** the animal. If they can extract enough DNA, the scientists could place it into the egg cells of a living elephant. If it works, the elephant would give birth to a woolly mammoth, bringing that long-dead species back from extinction.

CHAPTER 5

Learning From Fossils

You might be surprised at how much we can learn from fossils. More than just dusty bones, fossils are the keys to our planet's history. Fossils can tell us what animals and plants lived on Earth, when they lived, and many other things. They can tell us what Earth's geography and climate were like millions of years ago. They can even give us clues to the behavior of our human ancestors.

The Carboniferous period lasted from about 359 to 299 million years ago.

The Stories Bones Tell

The size of fossilized bones, of course, is a clue to the size of the animal. The size of a skull can give an idea of how large the animal's brain was. The size and shape of the teeth tell us if it ate plants or other animals. Footprints can help us estimate how heavy the animal was and whether it walked on all fours. Footprints also tell us whether it traveled alone or in groups.

The large, curved front teeth of the saber-toothed cat indicate that it hunted other animals for food.

It can be easy to spot the layers in sedimentary rock.

Knowing What Lived When

Imagine that you could slice through sedimentary rock from top to bottom and look at the layers within. Fossils near the bottom are the oldest. Those on upper layers are animals and plants that developed more recently. This is how paleontologists know that fish developed before reptiles and reptiles before mammals. Scientists can tell when an animal became extinct by seeing where its fossils are no longer found in the rock layers.

This fern fossil was found on Alexander Island in Antarctica.

Geography and Climate

Fossils can tell us what Earth was like long ago. The discovery of a fossilized fish on land shows that the area was once underwater. Finding similar fossils of land-dwelling organisms on two separate continents is a sign that those continents were once connected. Did you know that fossils of ferns and other warm-weather plants have been found in Greenland and Antarctica? This means that these icy regions were much warmer millions of years ago.

Our Human Ancestors

Certain animal fossils can even tell us about early humans. Scientists in Washington State recently made an exciting discovery. They found a mastodon rib with a spear point of sharpened bone lodged in it. The scientists determined the fossil is 14,000 years old. It is evidence that mastodons lived in the area during that time. It also shows that early humans made hunting tools out of bone. Who would believe that a fossil could tell us so much? ★

Early humans worked together to hunt mastodons and other large animals.

True Statistics

Length from nose to tail of *Argentinosaurus*, possibly the largest dinosaur that ever lived: 100 ft. (30.5 m)

Length of *Parvicursor*, one of the smallest dinosaurs that ever lived: 15 in. (38.1 cm)

Number of sharp, pointed teeth in the mouth of *Tyrannosaurus rex*: About 50

Age of *Eodromaeus murphi* and *Eoraptor lunensis*, the oldest dinosaurs ever found: 230,000,000 years

Number of years that cockroaches have lived on Earth: 350,000,000

Percentage of species that have ever lived on Earth that are alive today: Less than 0.1

Width of the antlers of the Irish elk, extinct for nearly 8,000 years: 12 ft. (3.7 m)

Did you find the truth?

(F) Scientists can learn about all the world's extinct animals by studying fossils.

(T) Dinosaurs had been extinct for more than 60 million years before humans first developed.

Resources

Books

Gray, Susan Heinrichs. *Paleontology: The Study of Prehistoric Life*. New York: Children's Press, 2012.

Greve, Tom. *Fossils: Uncovering the Past*. Vero Beach, FL: Rourke Publishing, 2011.

Lessem, Don. *The Kids Ultimate Dinopedia: The Most Complete Dinosaur Reference Ever*. Washington, DC: National Geographic, 2010.

Parker, Steve. *100 Things You Should Know About Fossils*. Broomall, PA: Mason Crest Publishers, 2011.

Visit this Scholastic Web site for more information on fossils:
★ www.factsfornow.scholastic.com
Enter the keyword **Fossils**

Important Words

clone (KLOHN) — to grow an identical plant or animal from the cells of another plant or animal

DNA (DEE EN AY) — the molecule found inside every cell in the body, containing information on how each cell should work

extinct (ik-STINGKT) — no longer found alive

fossil fuels (FOSS-uhl FYOOLZ) — coal, oil, or natural gas, formed from the remains of prehistoric plants and animals

fossilization (foss-uhl-ih-ZAY-shuhn) — the process of turning into a fossil

fossils (FOSS-uhlz) — bones, shells, or other traces of animals or plants from millions of years ago, preserved as rock

paleontologists (pay-lee-uhn-TAH-luh-jists) — scientists who study fossils to learn about ancient life-forms

petrified (PET-ruh-fide) — something that has become hard like stone because minerals have seeped into its cells

predators (PREH-duh-turz) — animals that live by hunting other animals for food

sedimentary rock (sed-uh-MEN-tur-ree RAHK) — rock formed from many layers of sediment that have been pressed together

Index

Page numbers in **bold** indicate illustrations

About the Author

Ann O. Squire is a psychologist and an animal behaviorist. Before becoming a writer, she studied the behavior of rats, tropical fish in the Caribbean, and electric fish from Central Africa. Her favorite part of being a writer is the chance to learn as much as she can about all sorts of topics. In addition to *Gemstones*, *Fossils*, *Rocks*, and *Minerals*, Dr. Squire has written about many different animals, from lemmings to leopards and cicadas to cheetahs. She lives in Katonah, New York.